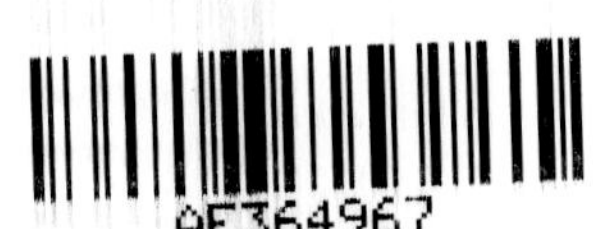
AF364967

an put a blank sheet between

the pages.

ck out my Instagram and TikTo

ccounts for nice tutorials how to

color the flowers.

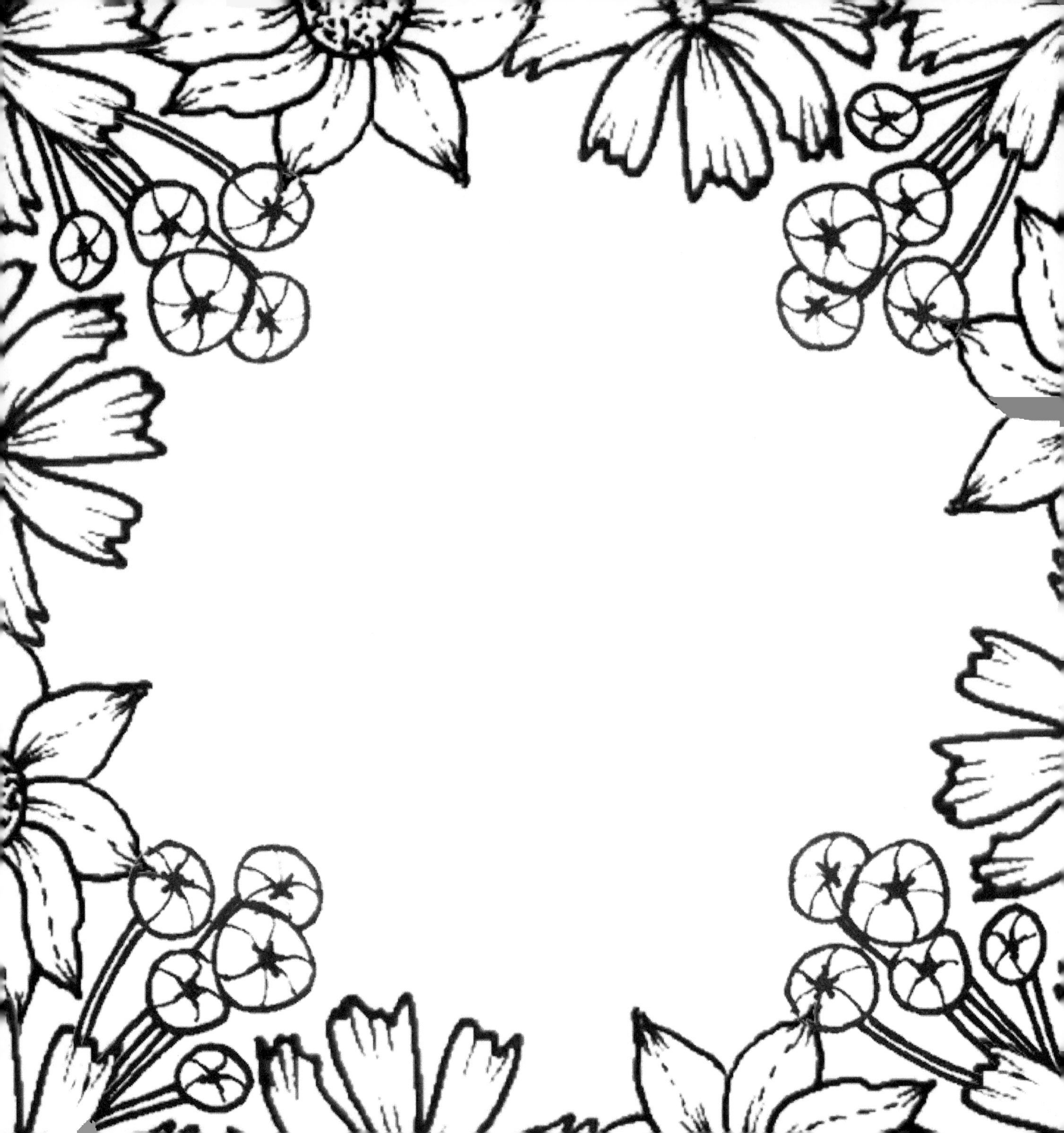

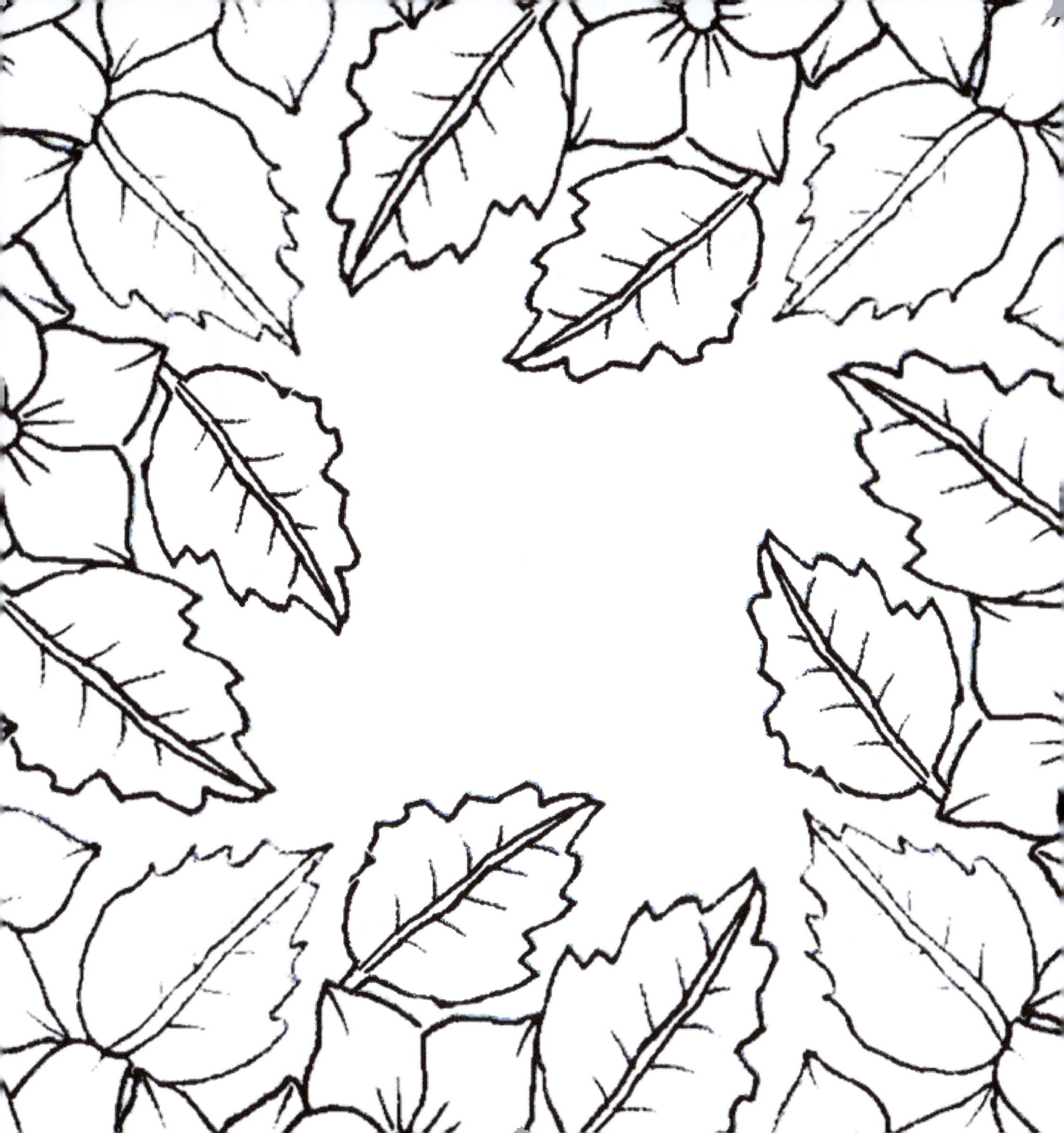

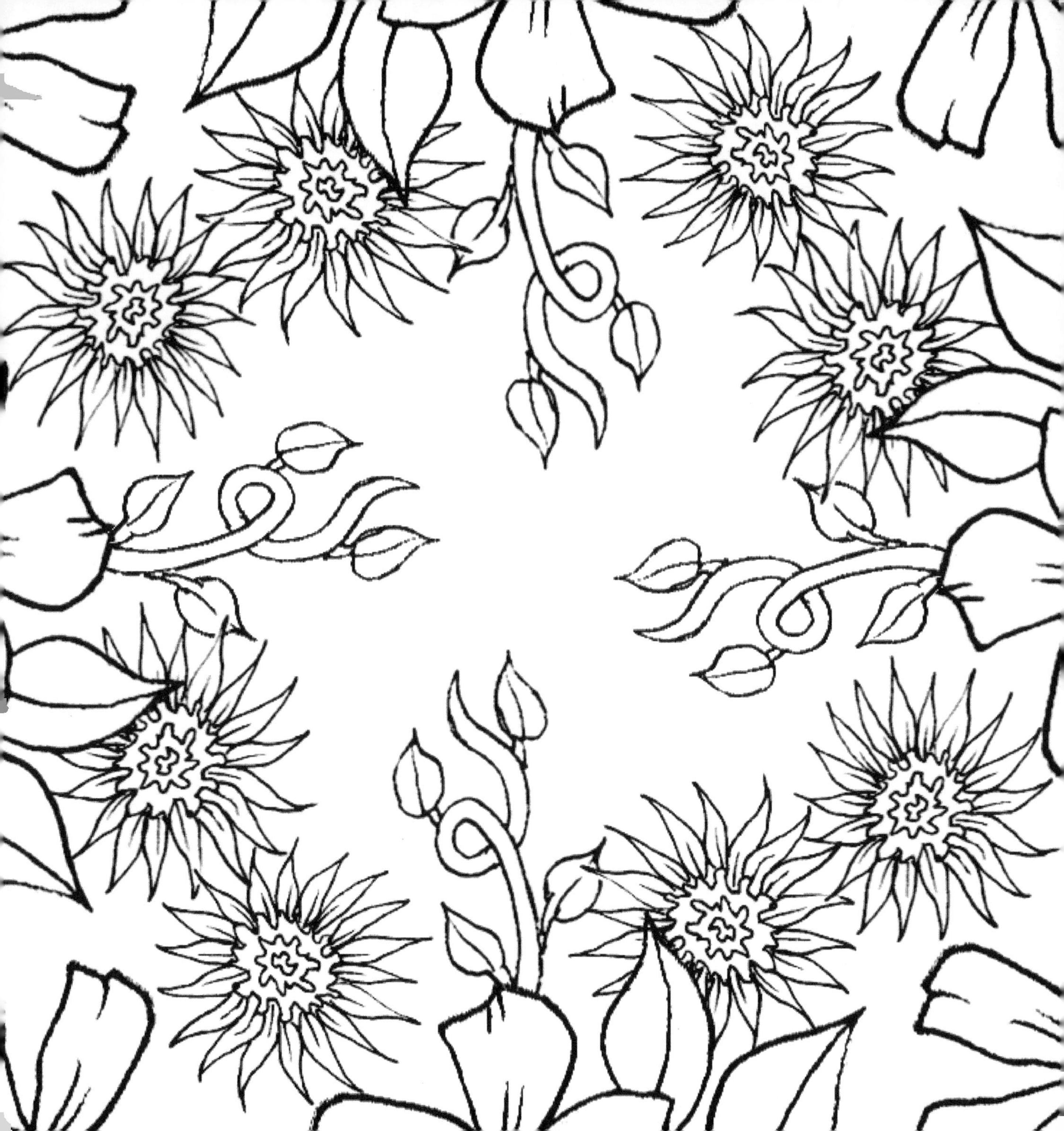

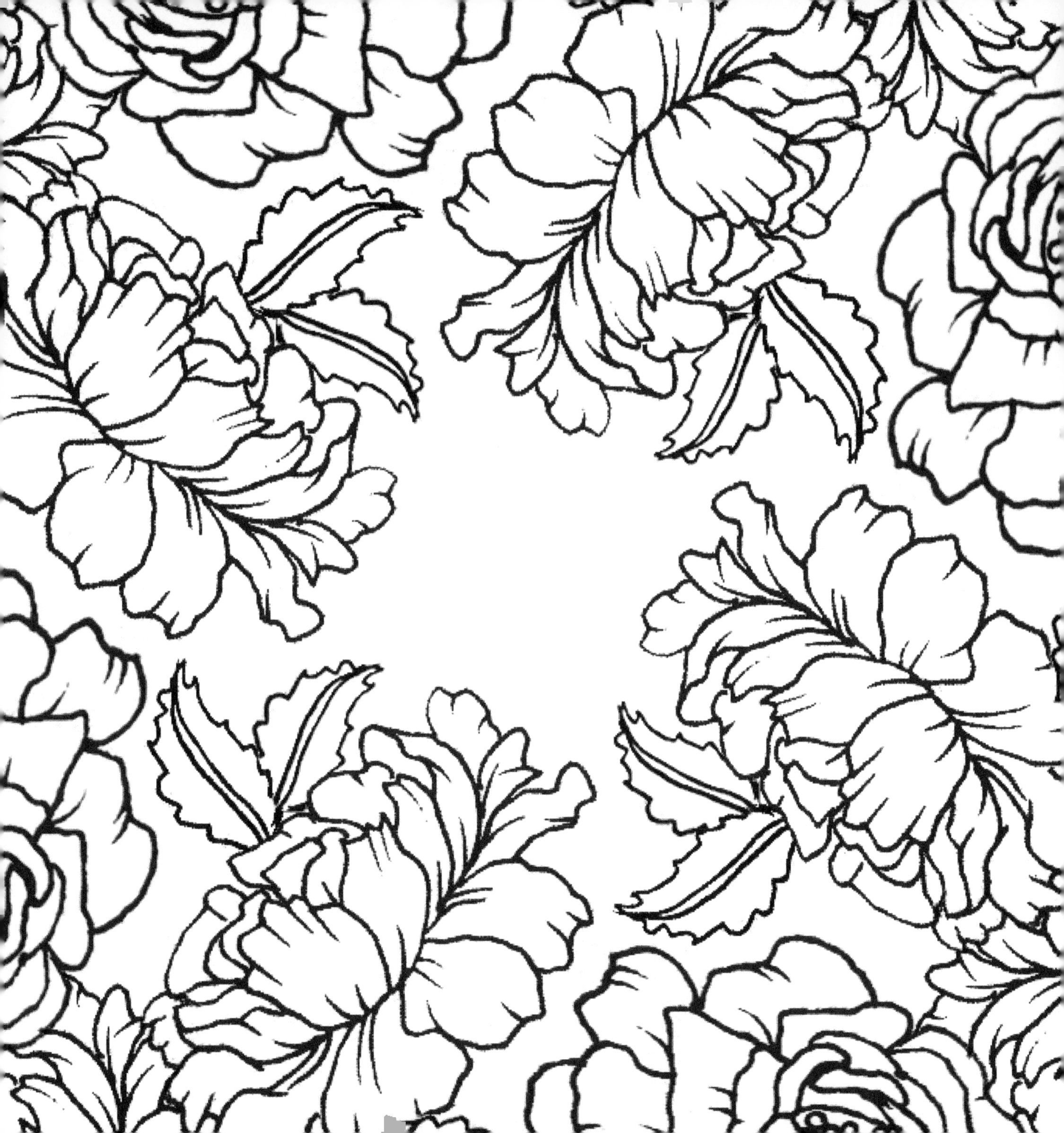

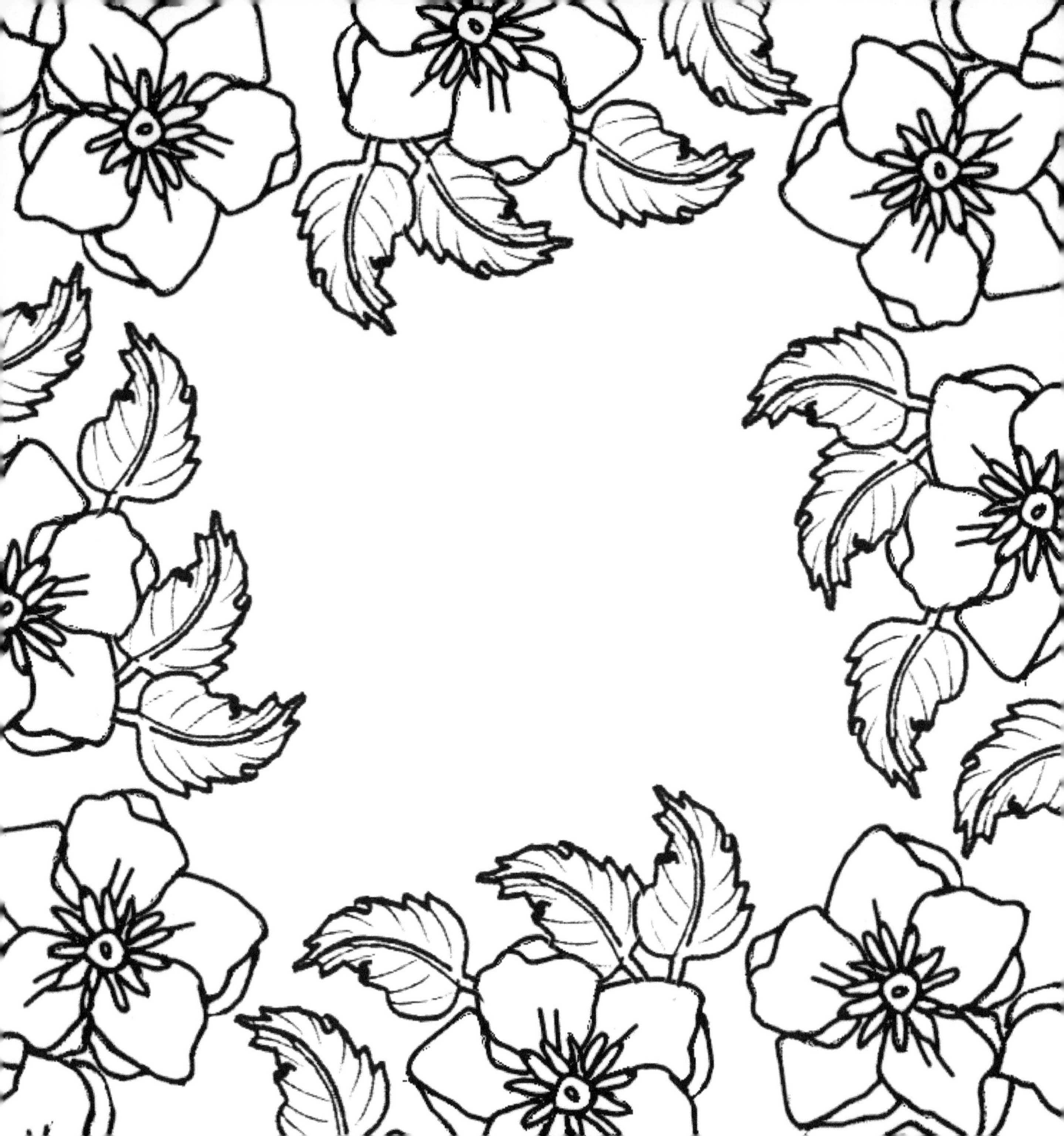

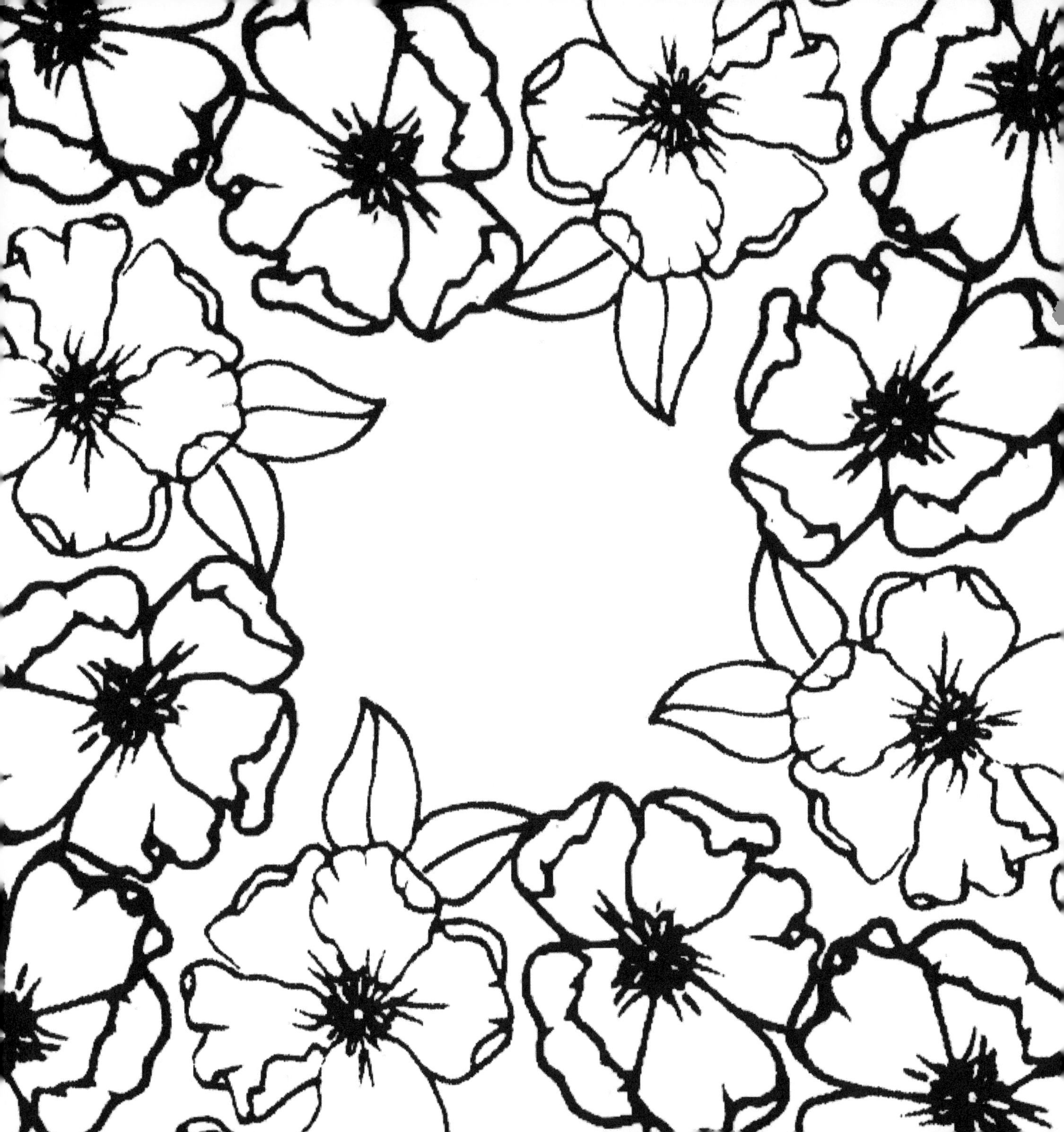

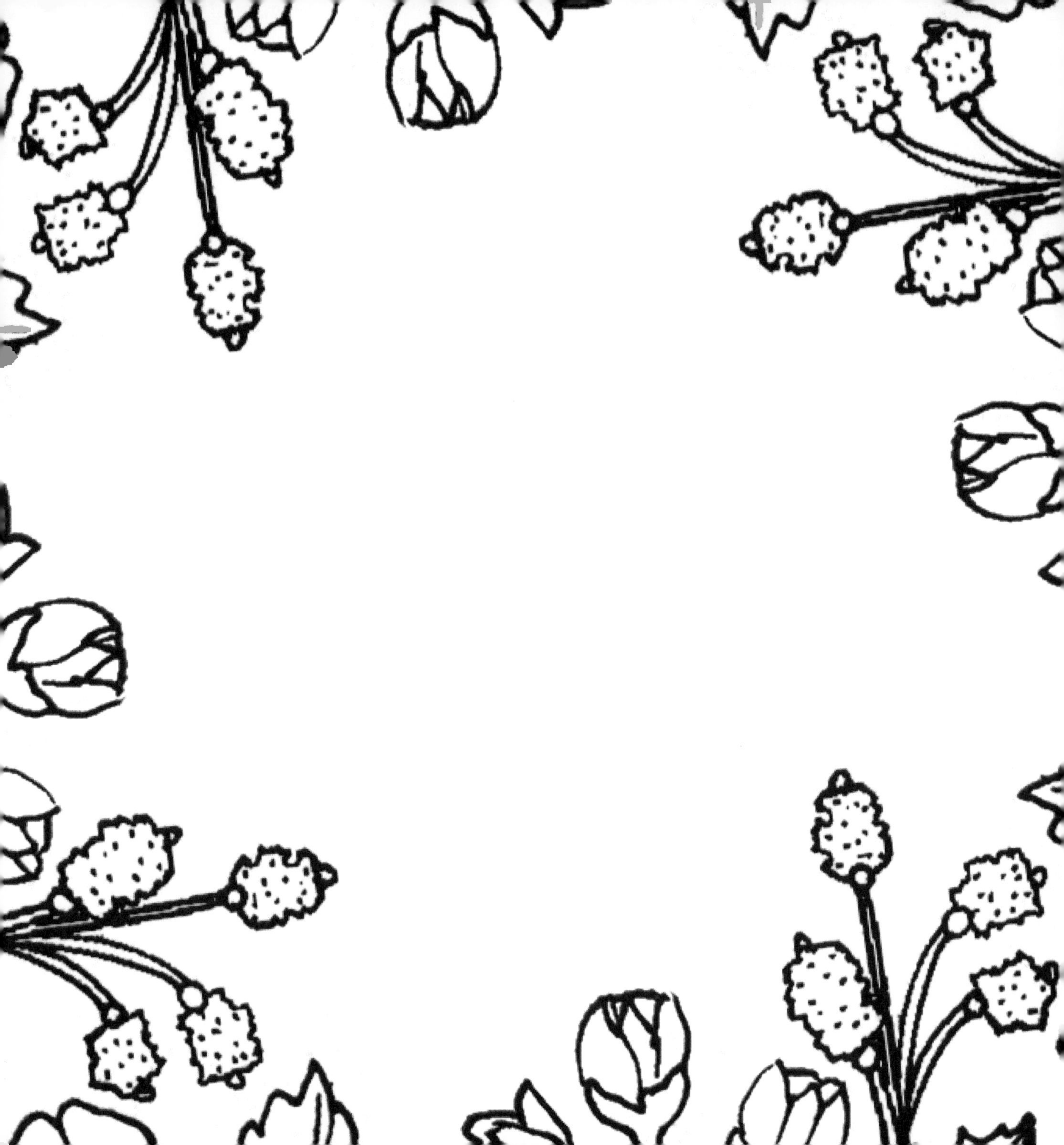

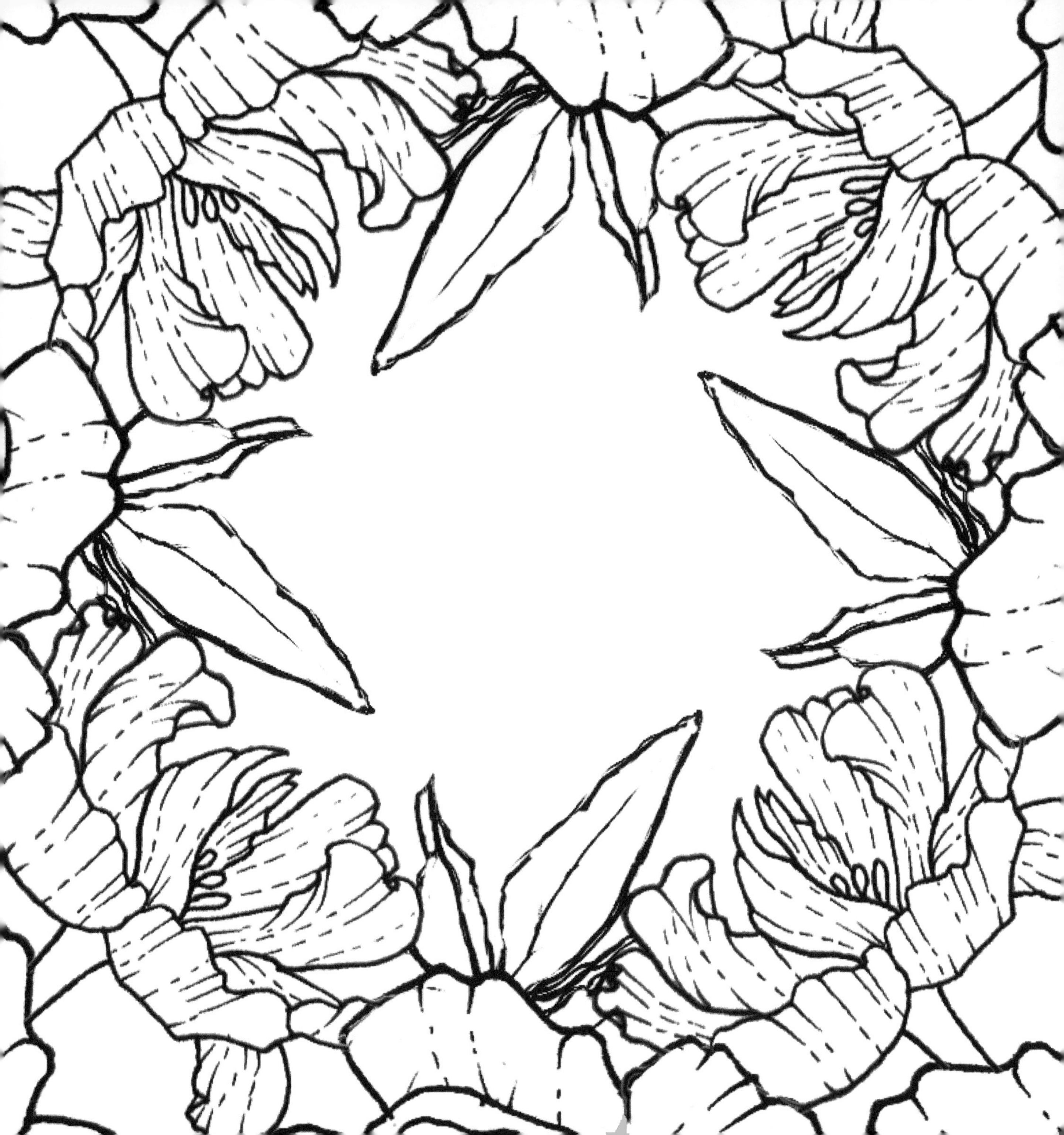

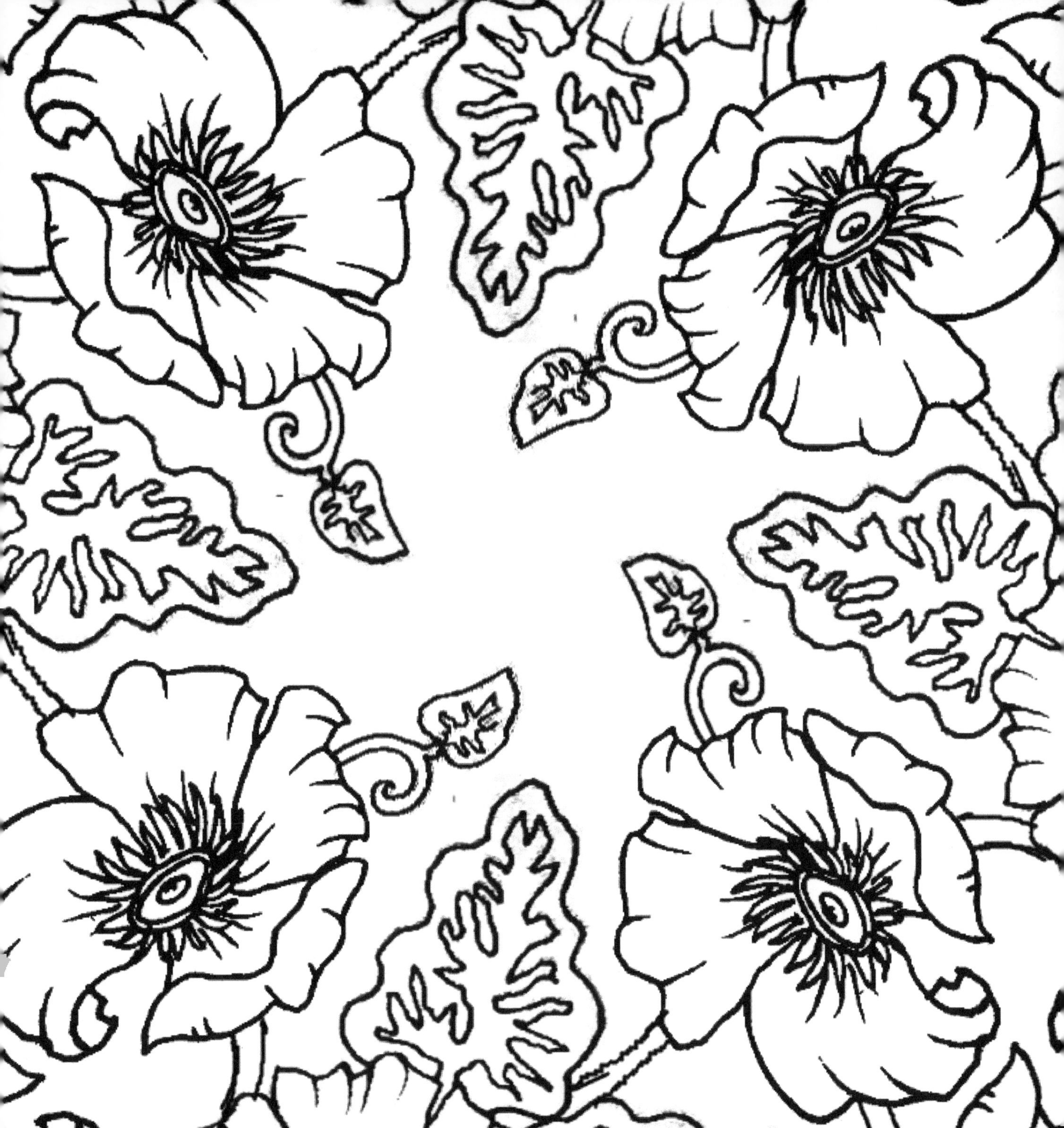

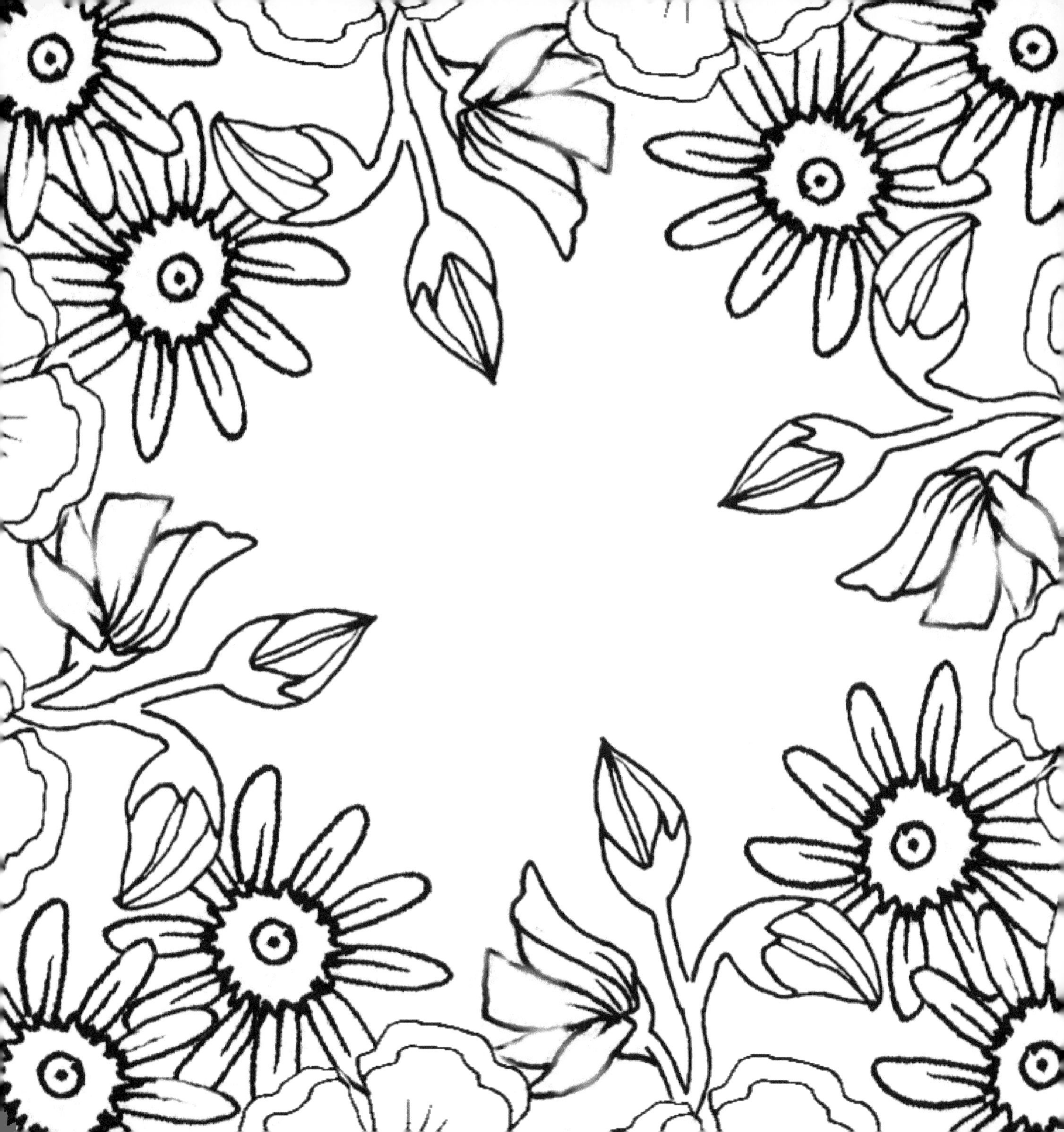

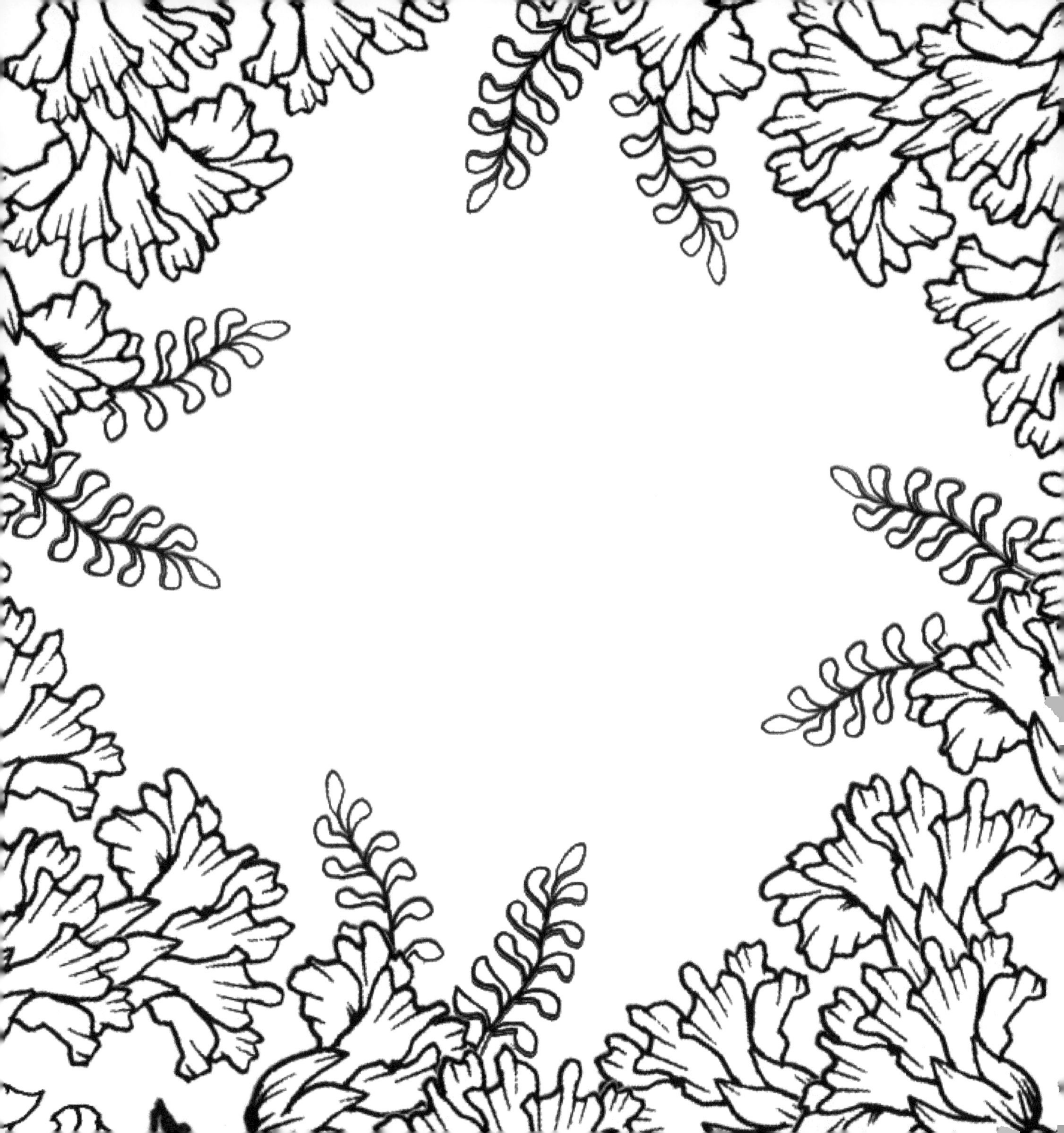

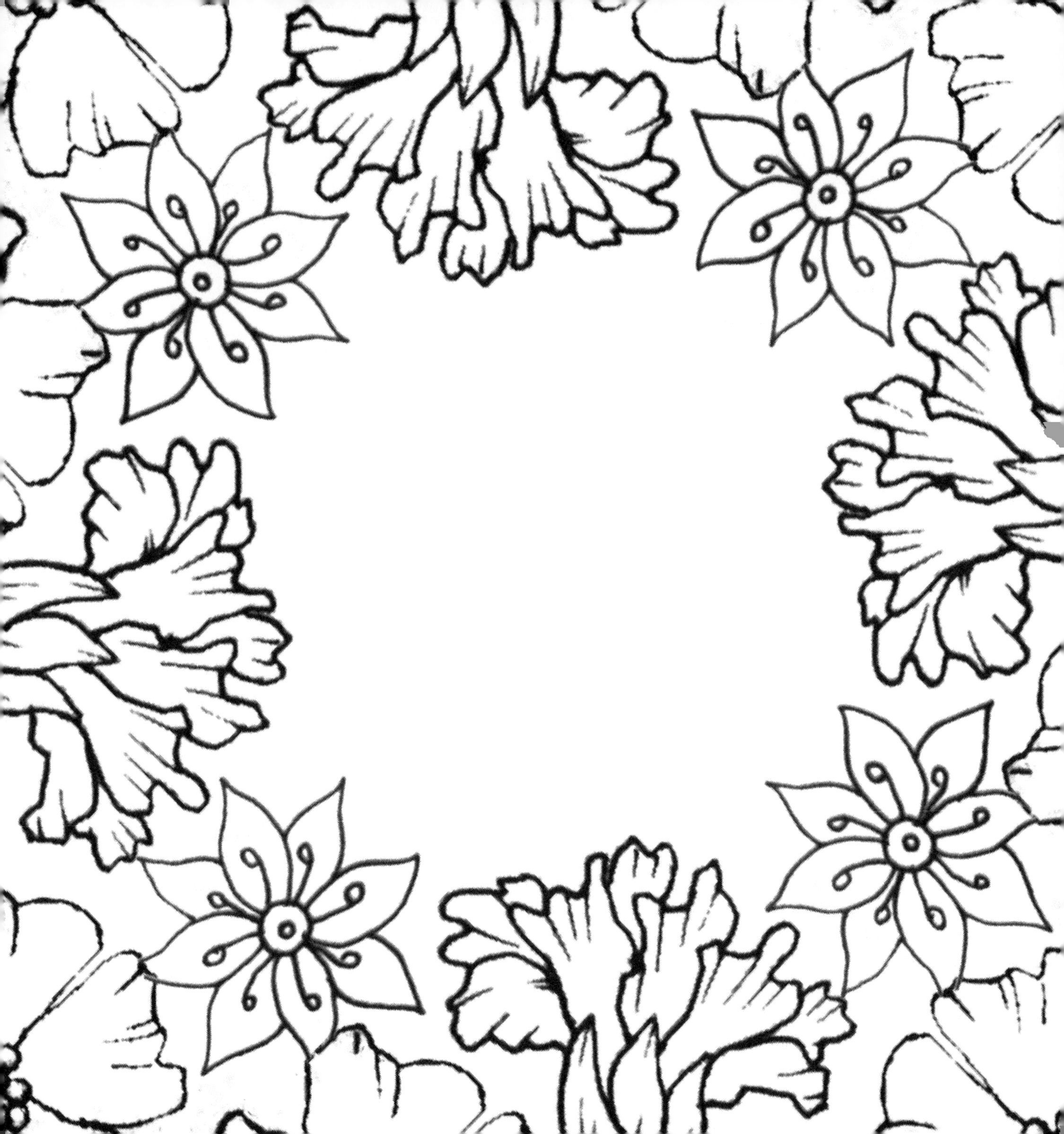

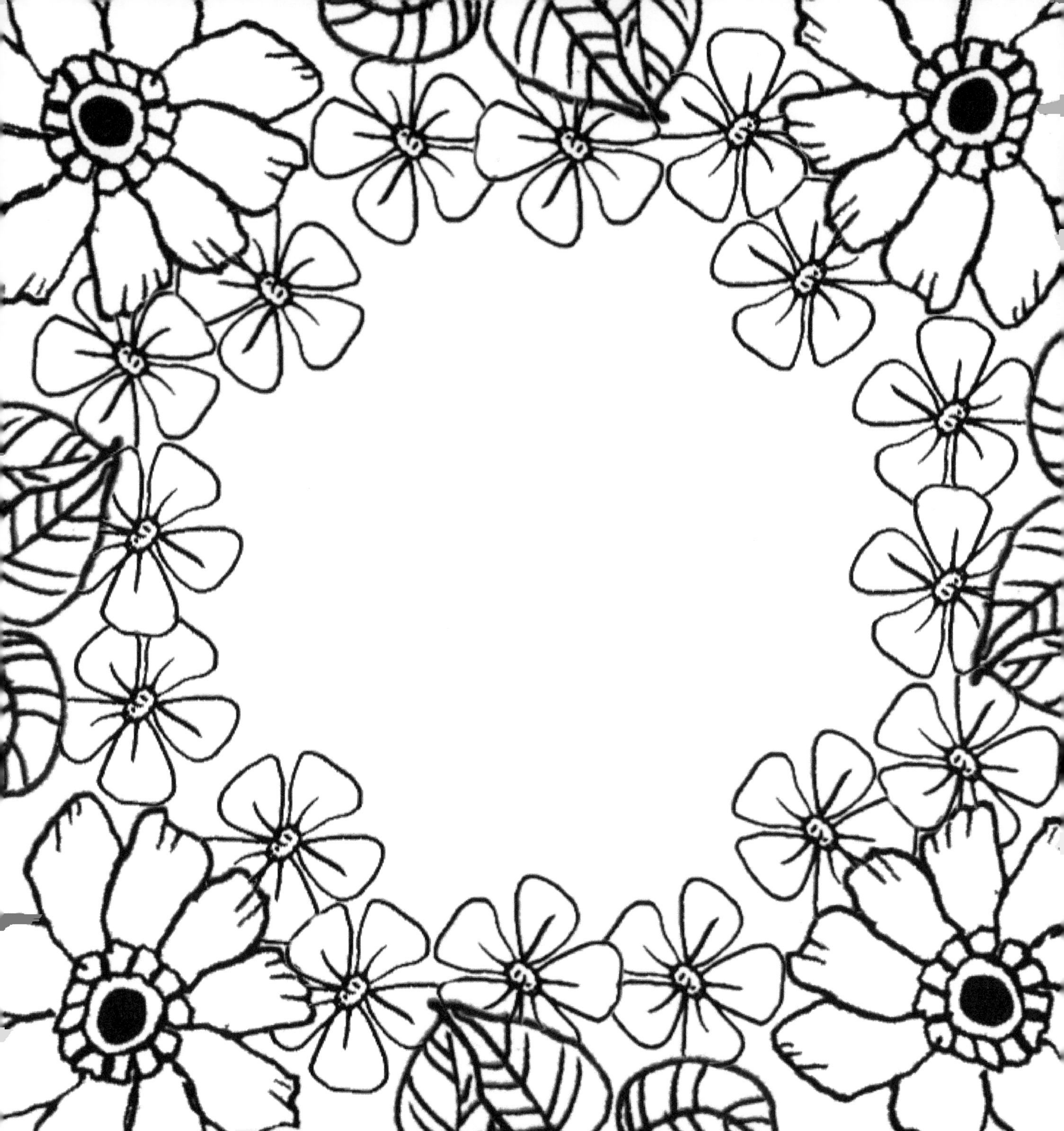

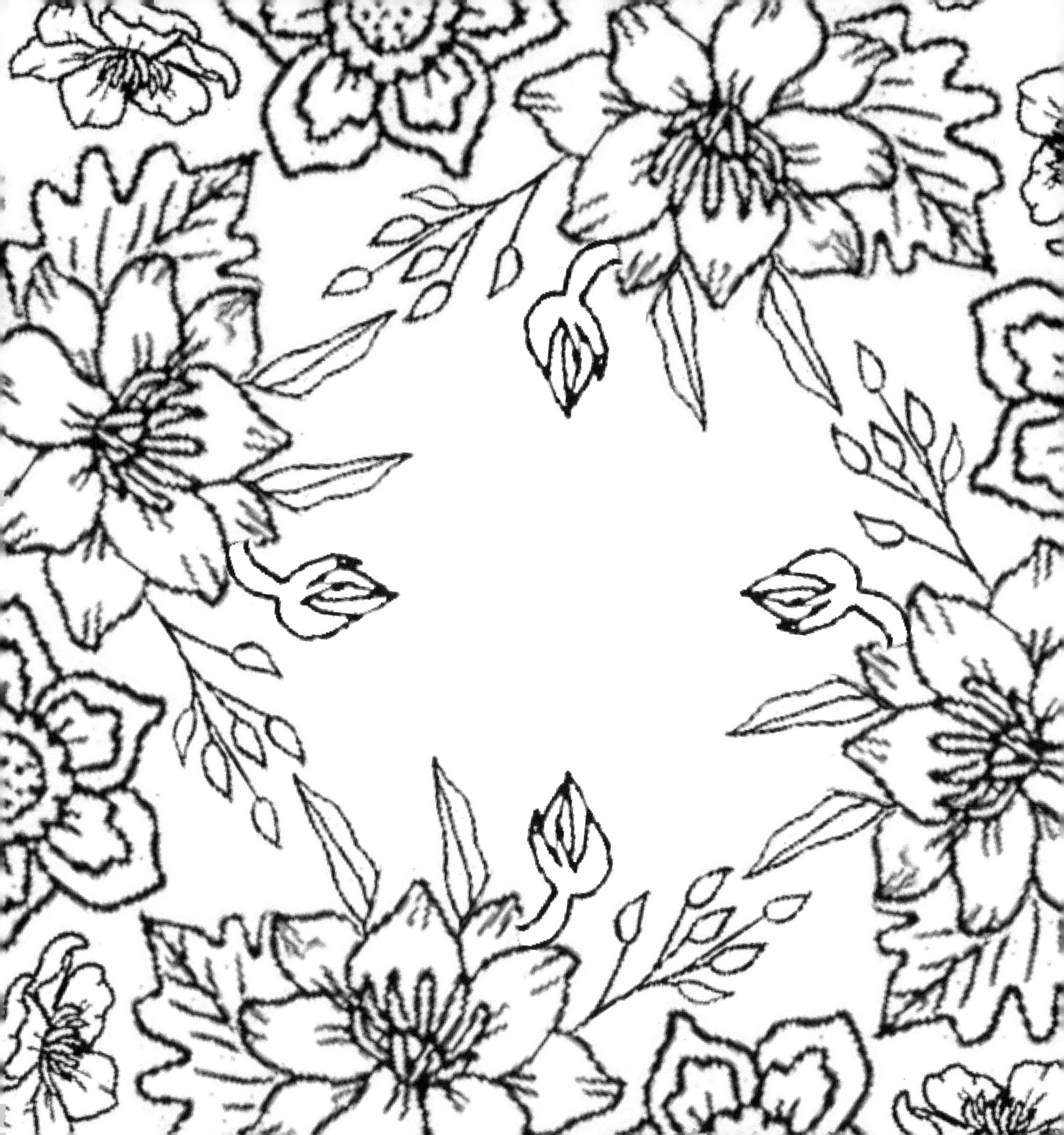

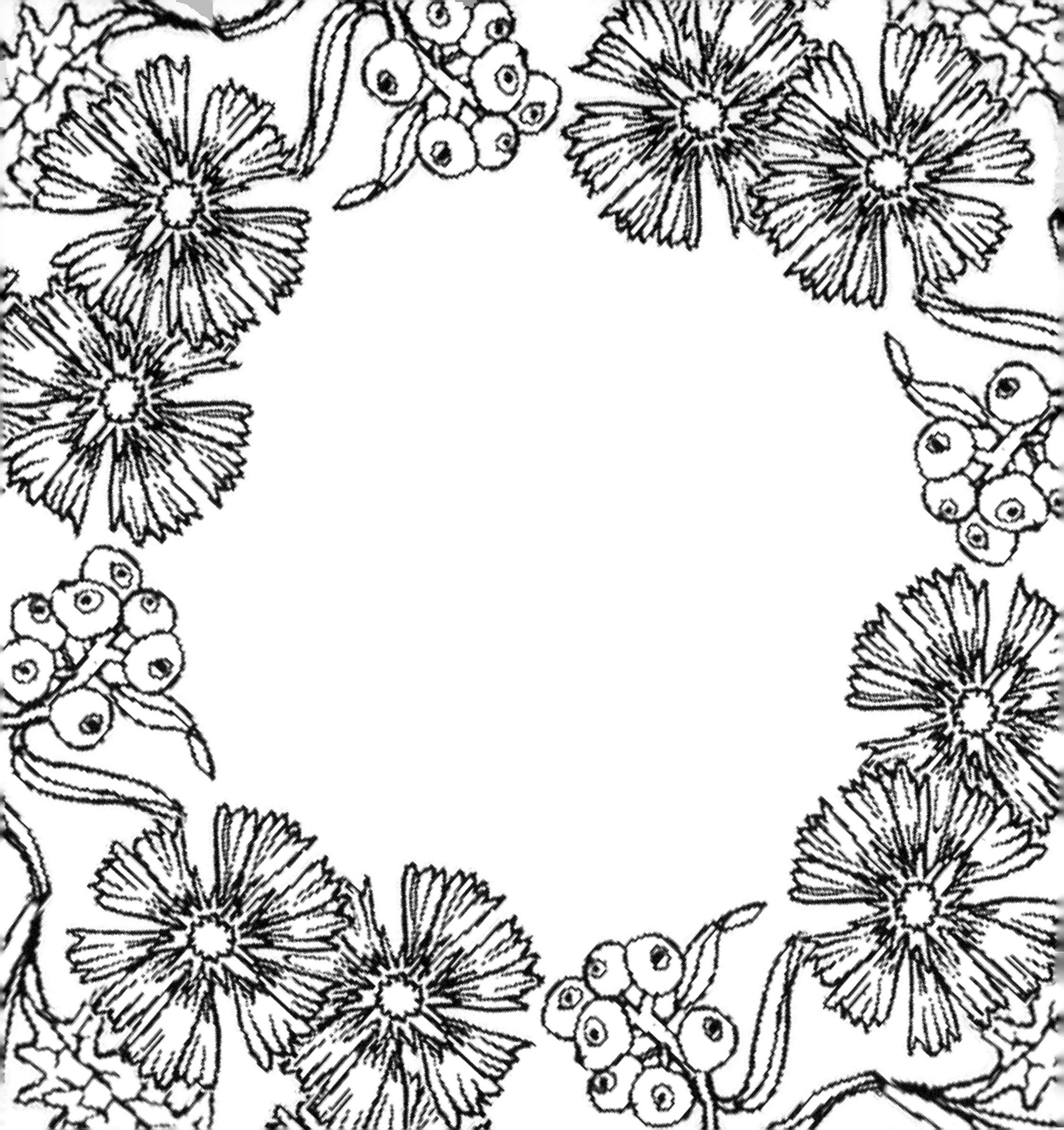

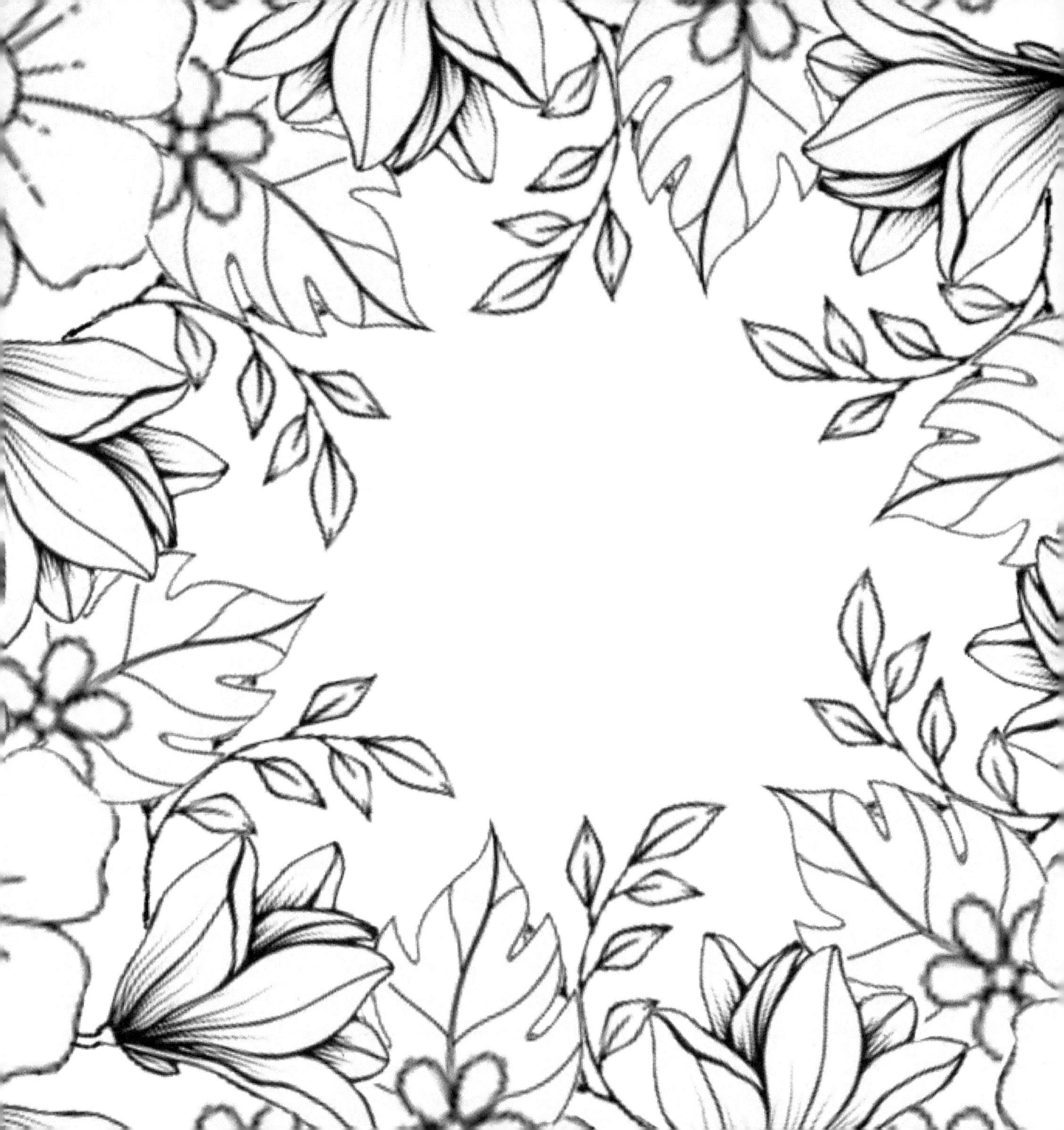

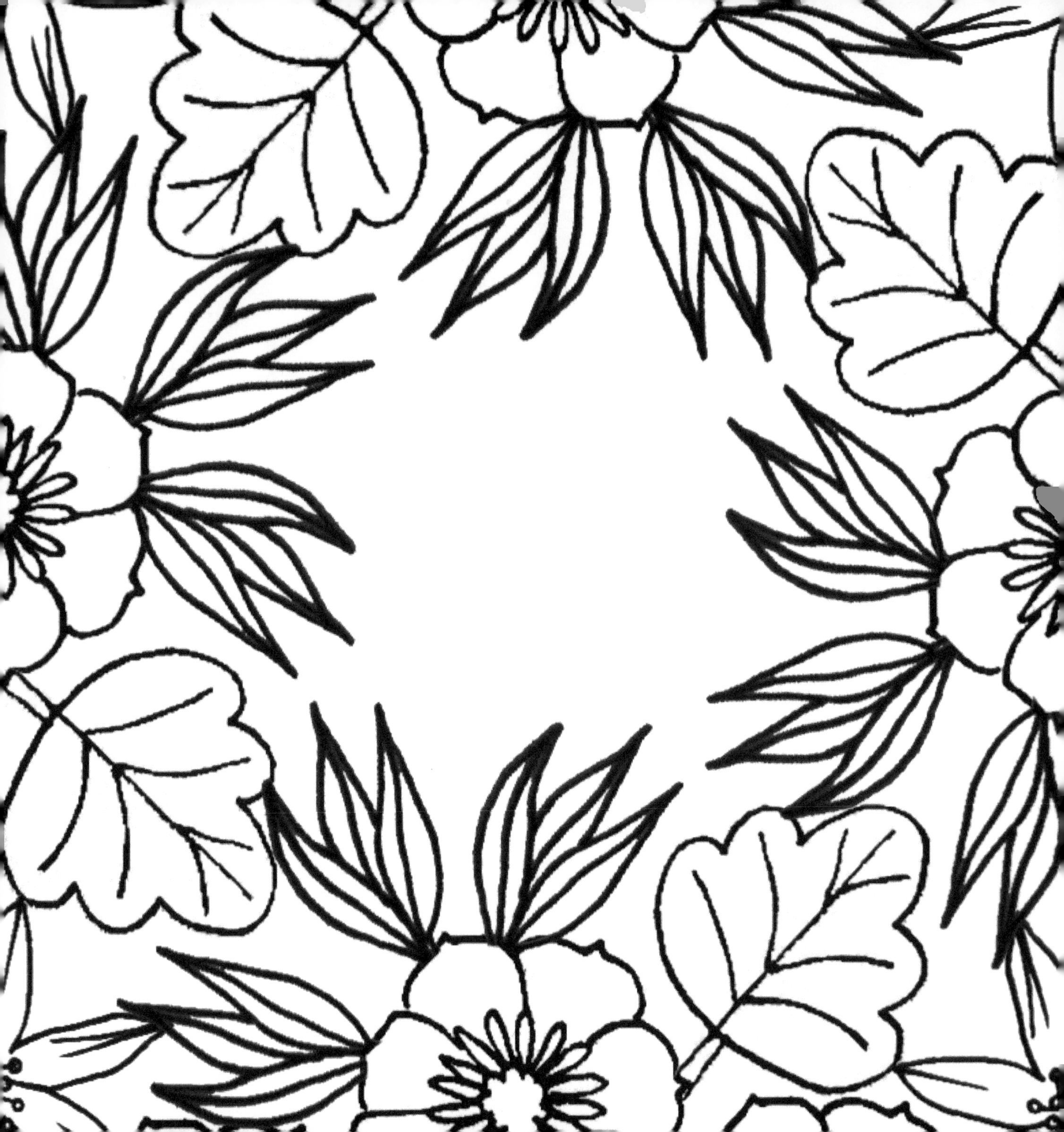

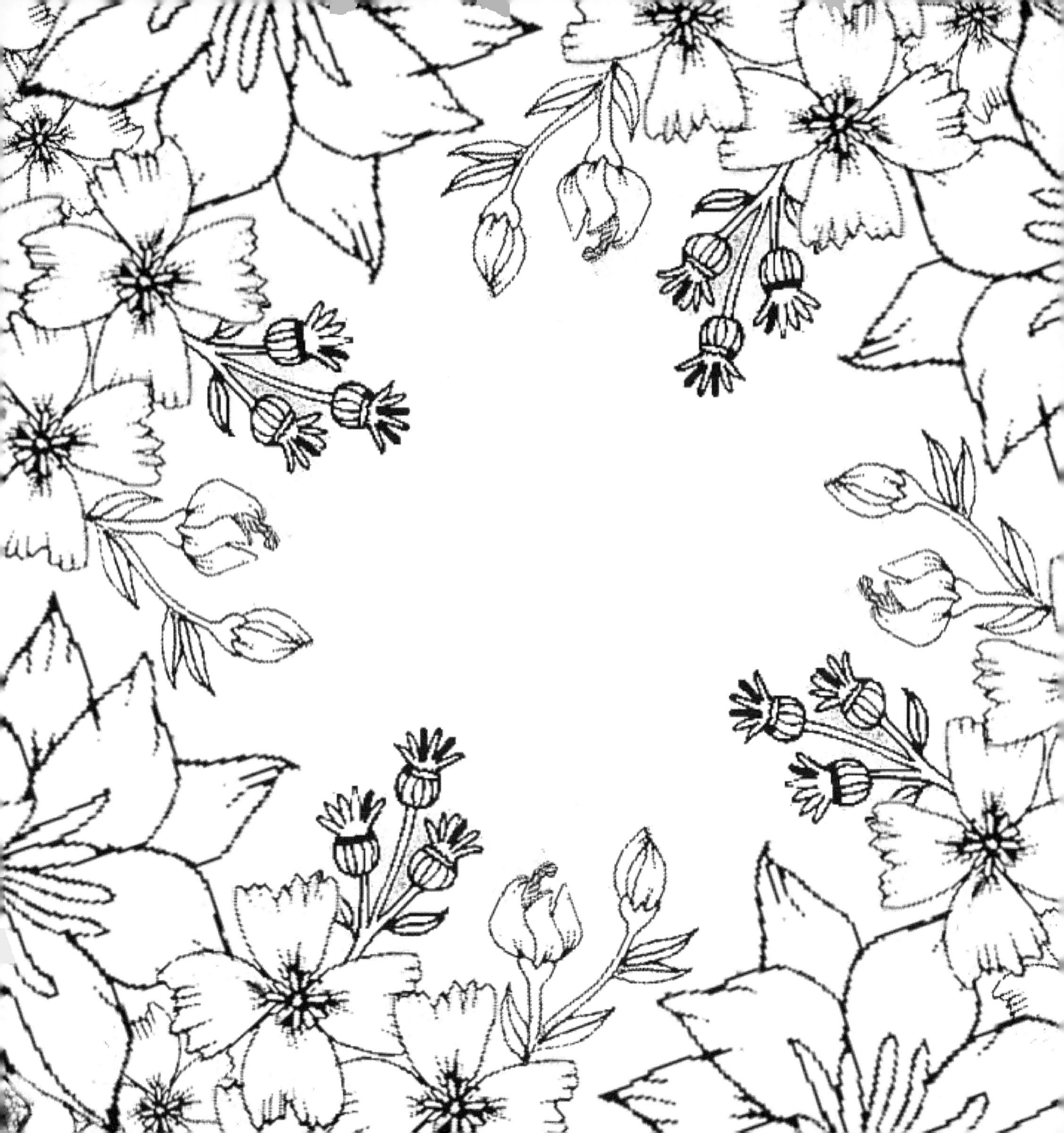

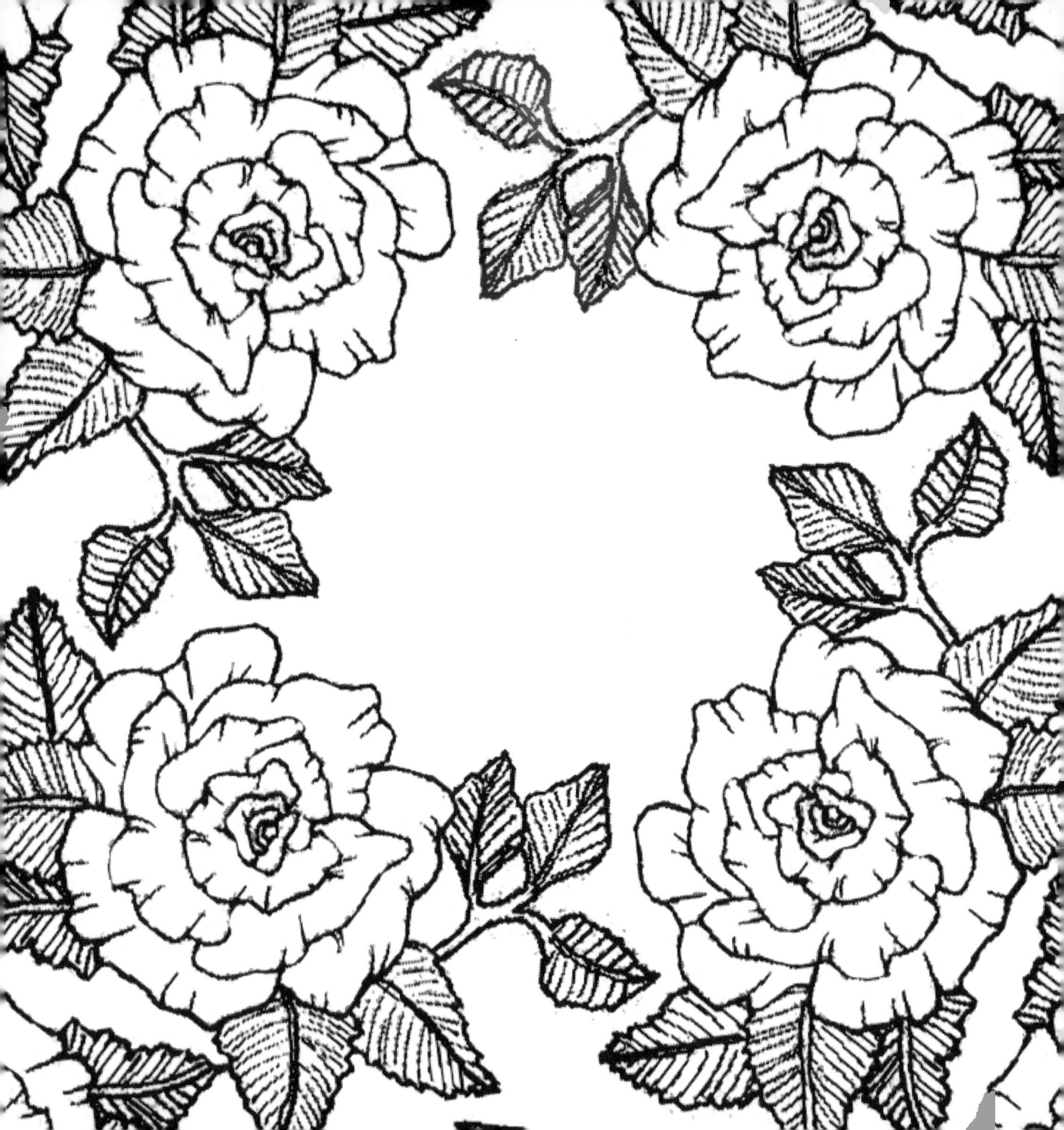

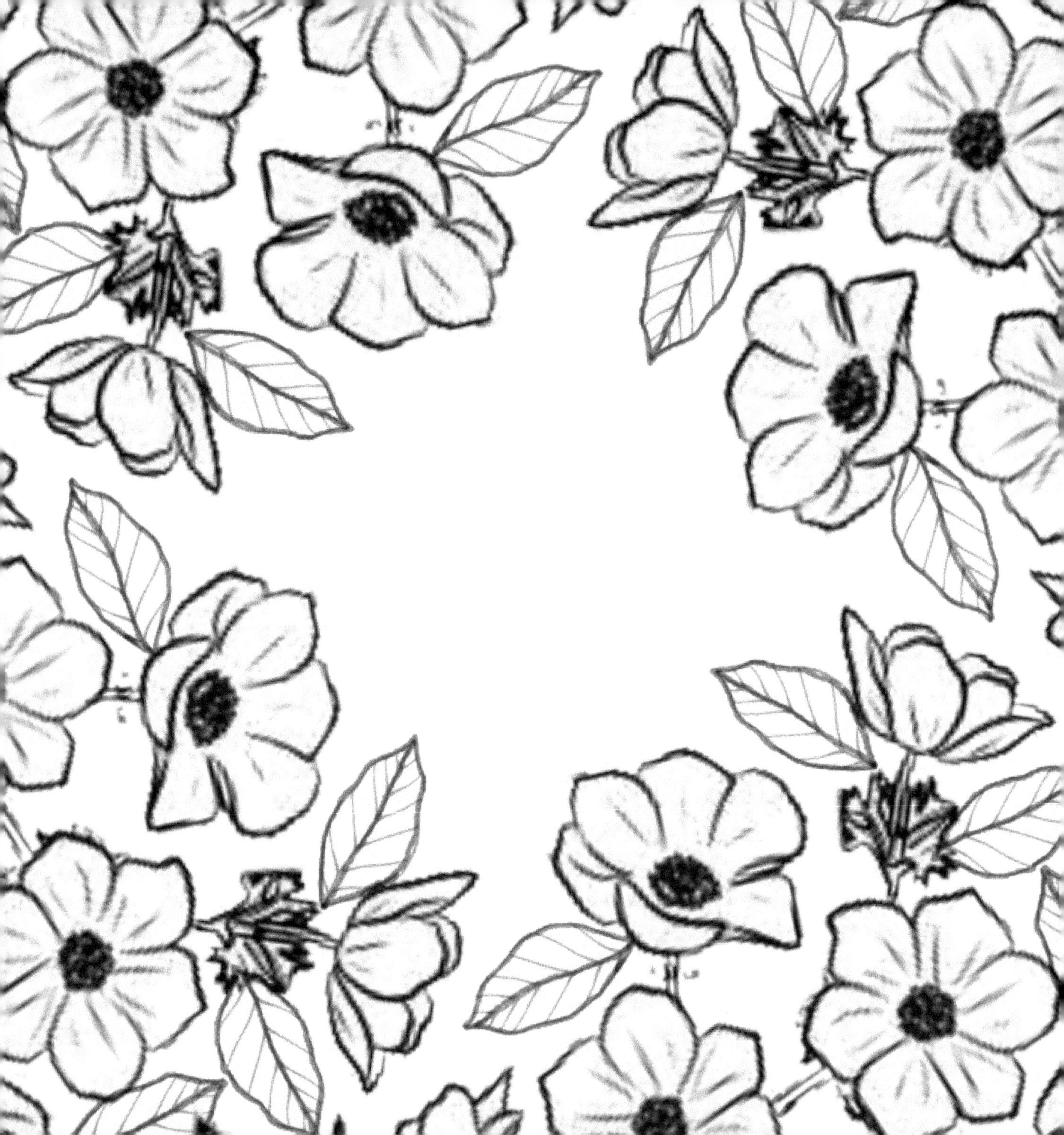

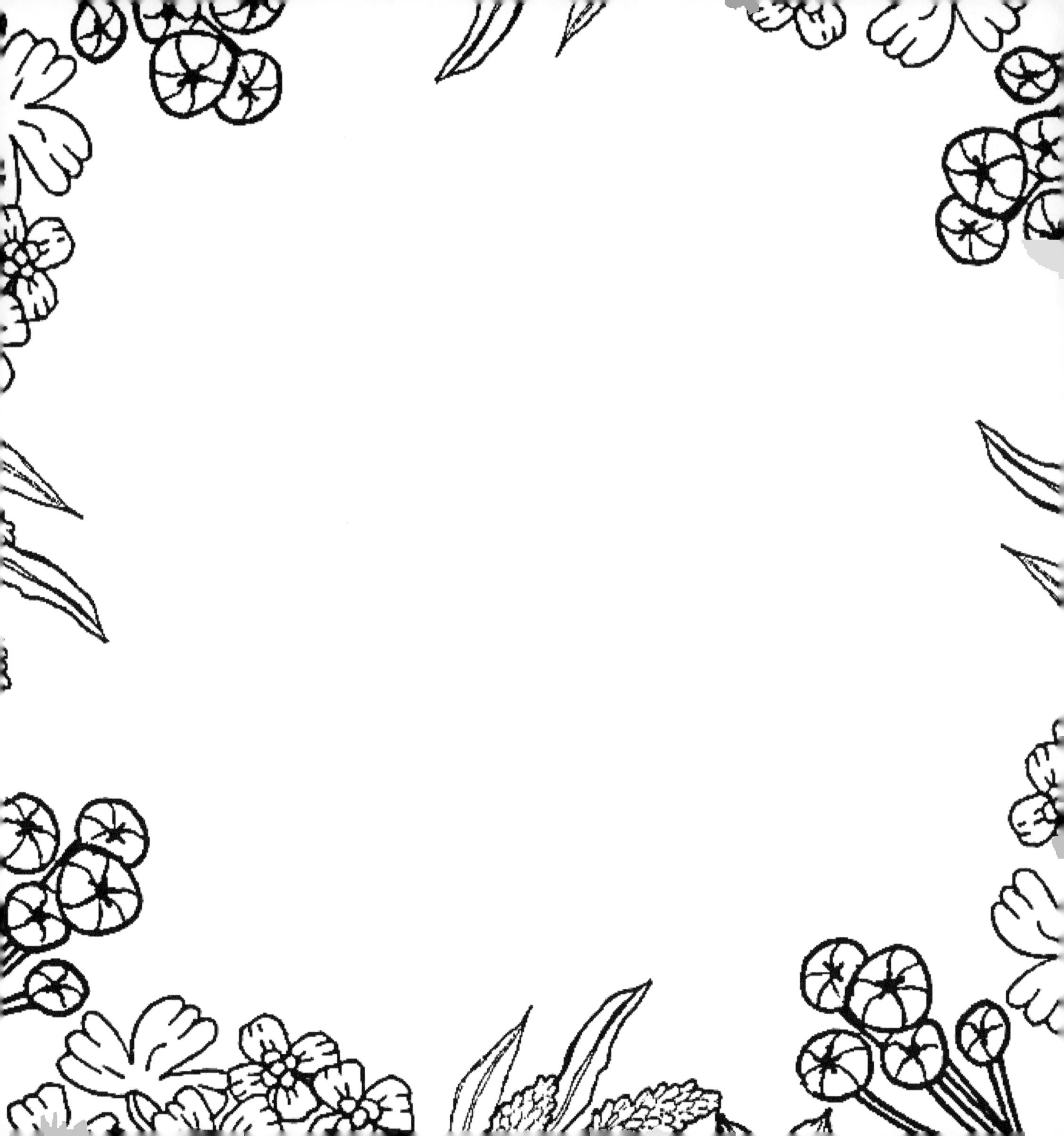

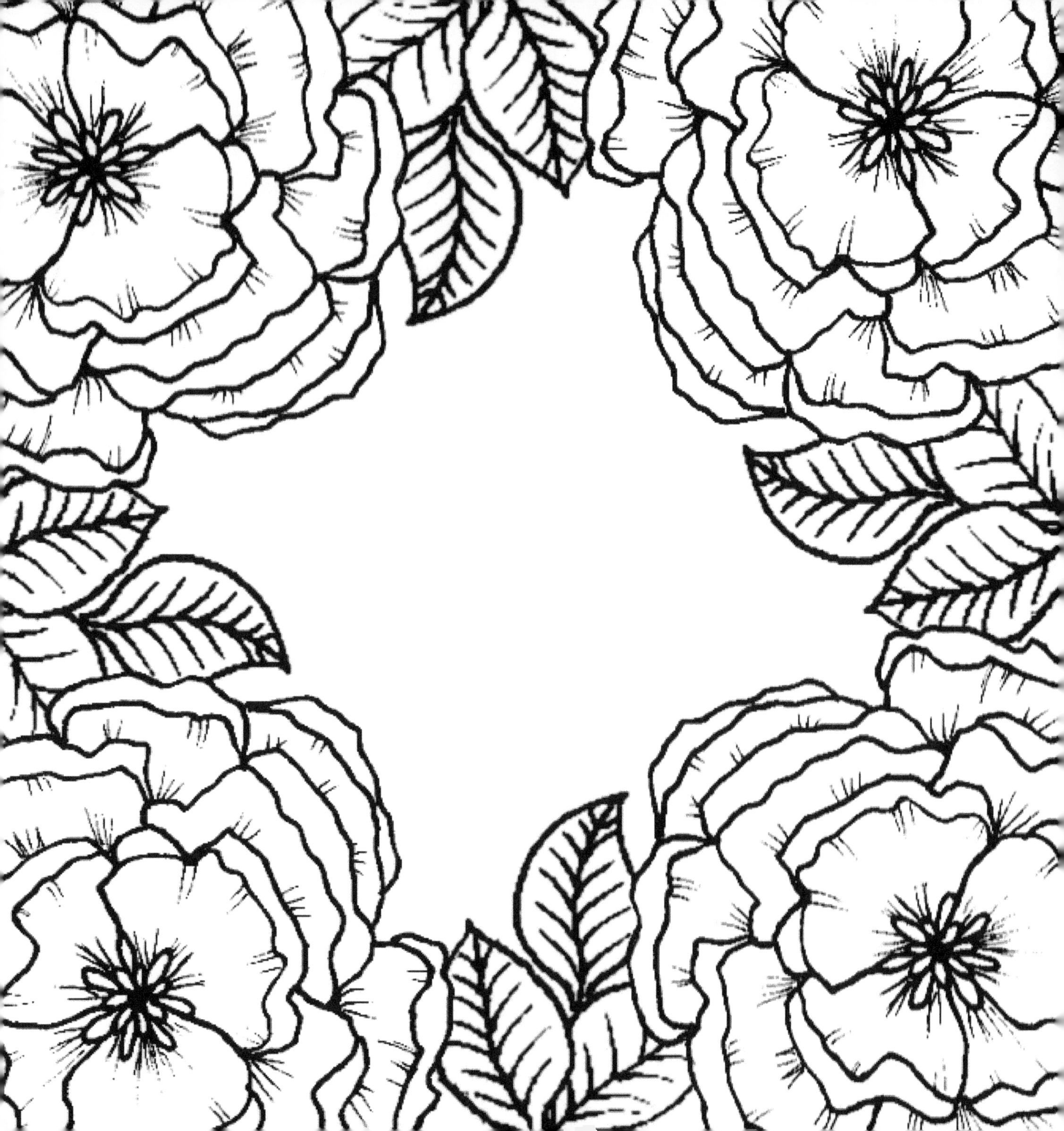

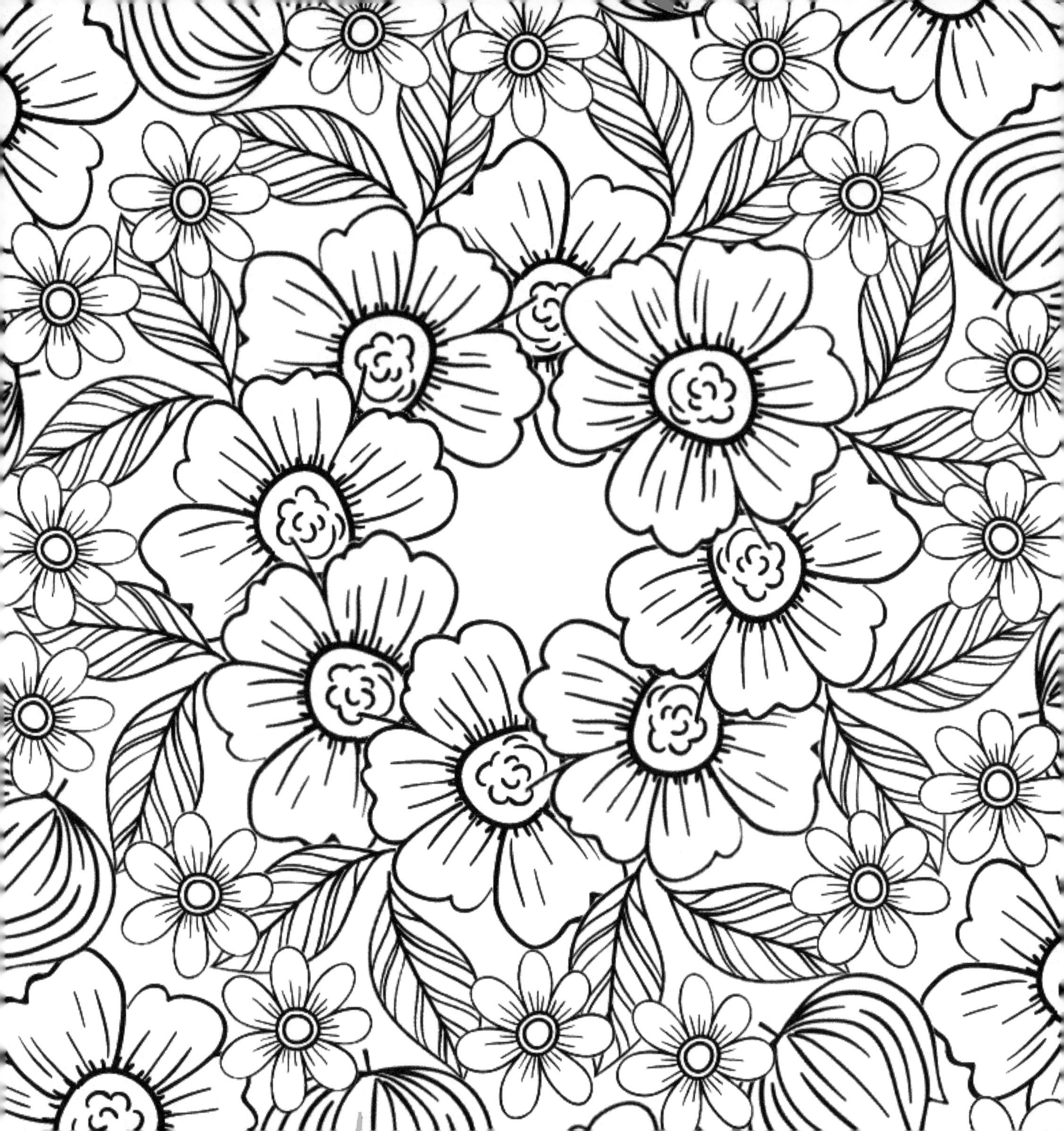

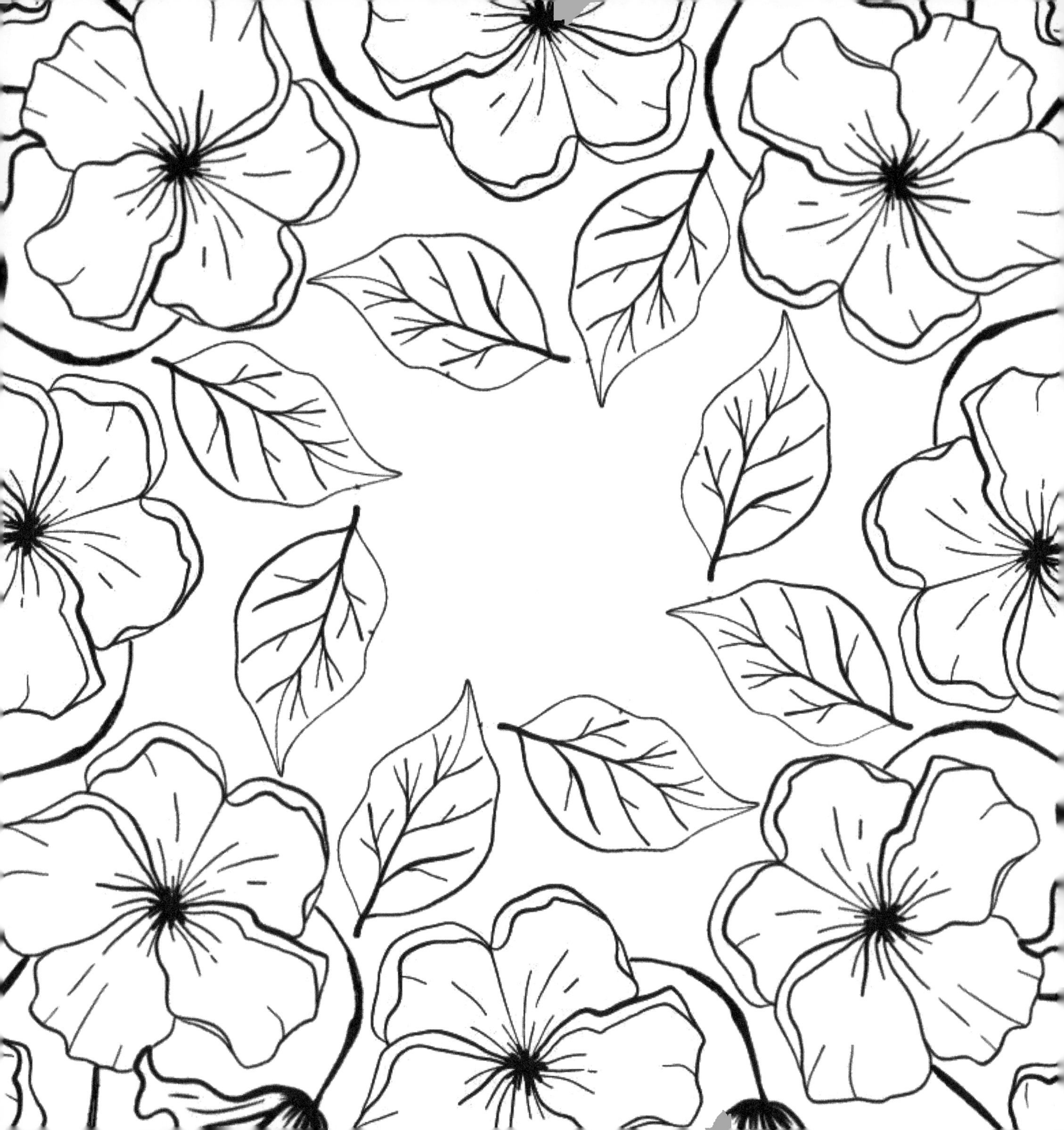

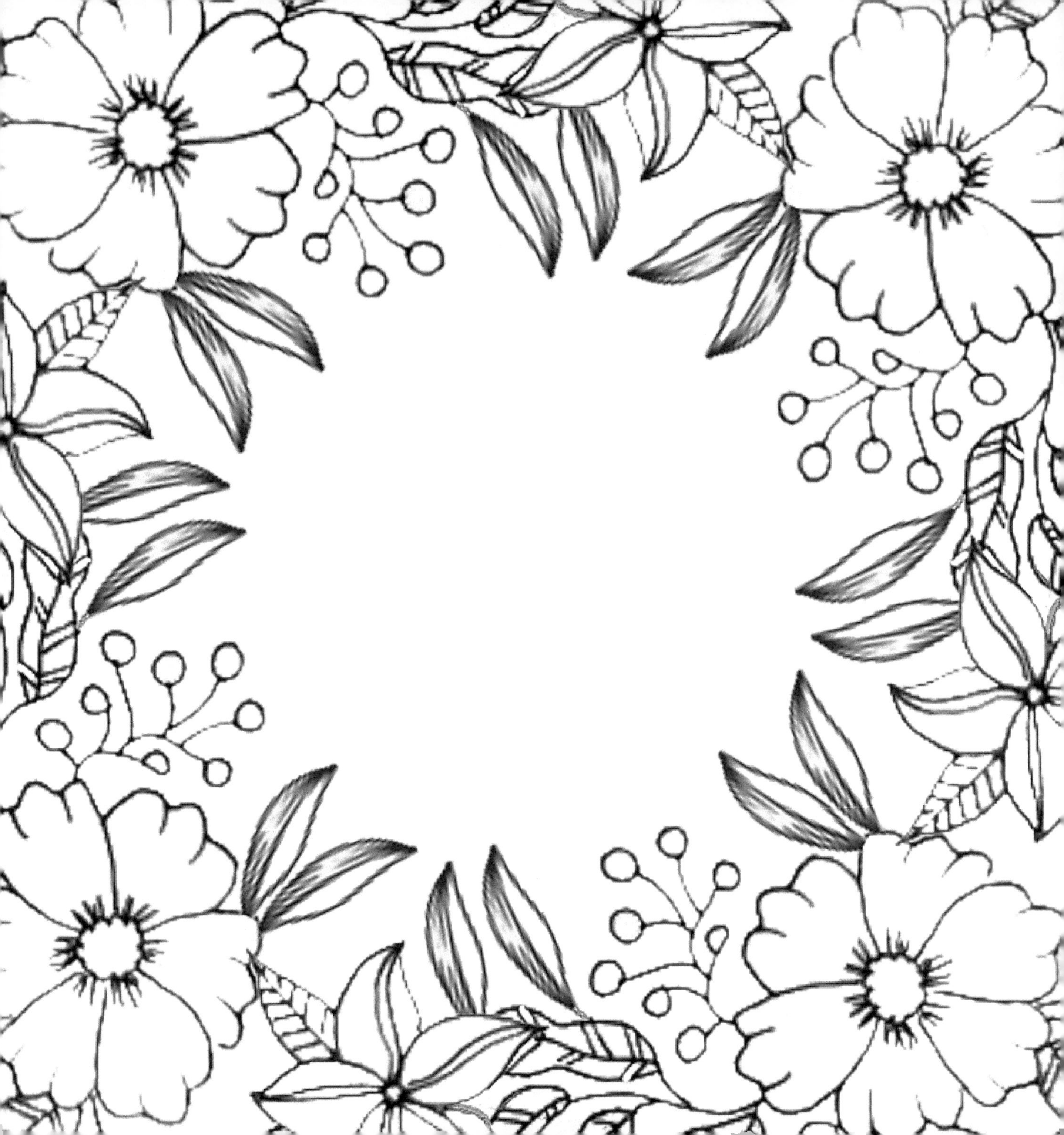